Join me on a woodland adventure, and explore this leafy collection of pen-and-ink illustrations all waiting to be brought to life through color.

Follow each shady trail as it winds through the forest to discover worlds filled with imagination and wonder. Fairy tales and woodland creatures can be found within, all drawn with a generous twist of fantasy and fun. For artists, wanderers, and nature lovers of all ages.

See more at rjhampson.com

 russelljamesart

Published by Hop Skip Jump
PO Box 1324 Buderim Queensland Australia 4556

First published 2022.
Copyright © 2022 R.J. Hampson.

All Rights Reserved. Without limiting the rights under copyright reserved above, no part of this publication may be reproduced, stored in or introduced into a retrieval system, or transmitted, in any form or by any means (electronic, mechanical, photocopying, recording or otherwise), without the prior written permission of both the copyright owner and the above publisher of this book. The only exception is by a reviewer who may share short excerpts in a review.

ISBN: 978-1-922472-22-9

Using this book

Find a quiet place away from distractions. Relax and immerse yourself in the process of coloring as you explore the details of each illustration.

This book is best suited to color pencils or markers. Wet mediums should be used sparingly. Slide a card or sheets of paper behind the illustration you are coloring to avoid marker bleed through.

Find fresh coloring pages by signing up to Russell's newsletter. Get free downloadable pages and updates on new books at -

rjhampson.com

FALL

MR FOGHERTY TAKES A BREAK

A CACOPHONY OF COCKATOOS

THE BIRDS

RED

THE FOREST KINGDOM

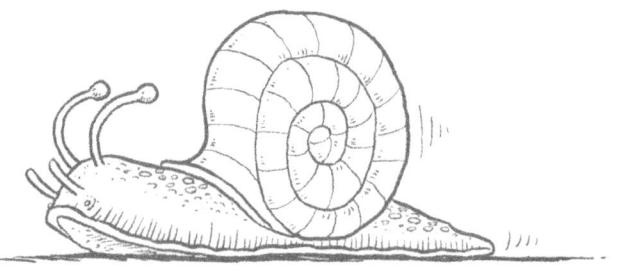

PORTOBELLO ROAD

SUMMER

TEMPTATION

A RIVER RUNS THROUGH IT

SUNDAY MORNING

WINTER

LOTUS DREAMS

SPRING

THE SWORD IN THE STONE

THE DORMICE

BESIDE THE LAKE, BENEATH THE TREES

THE LUMBERJACK

THE GUARDIAN

FOXY TROUBLE

PHOENIX TREE

PHOENIX TREE

WITH THE HEART OF MAY

LULLABY

BENEATH AN EVENING MOON

LOST TEMPLE

Searching for more?

Find new coloring pages by signing up to Russell's newsletter.
Get free downloadable pages, monthly coloring sheets,
and updates on new books at -

rjhampson.com/coloring

Thanks for choosing this coloring book.
If you enjoyed it, please consider leaving a review.
It will help to let more people in on the experience
plus you'd certainly make this illustrator very happy!

Published books in this series

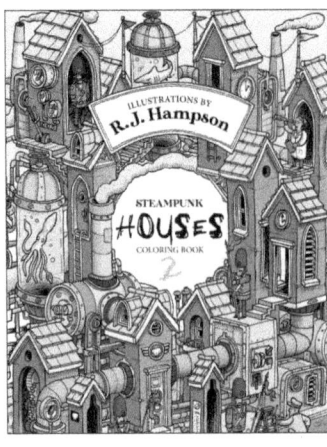

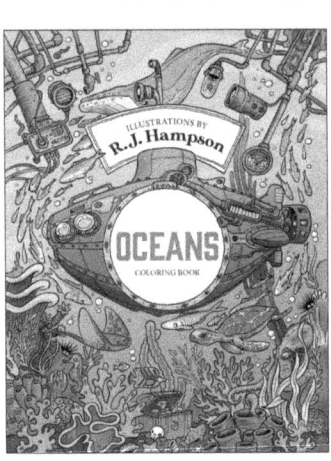

See flip-throughs and new releases at **rjhampson.com**

www.ingramcontent.com/pod-product-compliance
Lightning Source LLC
Chambersburg PA
CBHW041221240426
43661CB00012B/1105